# MANNA ON ACHIEVEMENT

*Focus On Achievement With Me For A Few Moments Today.*

It is one of the most fascinating subjects on earth. It is also one of the most distorted, perverted and misunderstood topics. In fact, many people continuously criticize unusual achievers. It may be jealousy, envy or conviction. I do not really know, but it is sad and unfortunate to hear the barrage of destructive words regarding workaholics.

Some ministers even take their scalpel and slice through the heart of those who are obsessed with *producing something significant in their daily routine.* Talk shows are filled with sneering comments about those obsessed with a *mission,* an Assignment, a consuming focus for their lives.

It is quite obvious. The masses of

average people consider those who are energized, enthusiastic and focused, to be flawed. They work *too* hard, achieve *too* much and are considered quite unbalanced.

Rarely is the *truth* carefully considered. It is the workaholic who normally signs the paychecks for others, sets the goals, establishes the pace and sees productivity as an *asset* in life.

Certainly, there are abuses and imbalances that must be considered. But it is interesting how God first pictures Himself to humans.

It happens in the *first* book of the Bible. The *first* chapter. The *first* verse. He did not establish Himself as relationship-oriented, believe it or not! In His words, "In the beginning God created the Heaven and the earth," (Genesis 1:1).

He did not discuss His feelings.

He did not discuss His dreams and goals.

He discussed His work...His productivity...His accomplishments.

He said, "I am an *achiever.* I *do* things. I *create.* I *produce.* I set in motion. I am energized. I am not a do nothing, sit-on-my-rear-end kind of God." That is why the entire subject of achievement is worthy of our focus today.

The Holy Spirit is an *achiever*.

He reveals, imparts and *completes*.

He is an *enabler*.

It is true that some people become so involved in their work that their family life is forgotten, neglected and deteriorated.

It is also true that many people sit in their homes and deteriorate with their family rotting, dying around them.

Just a brief word concerning achieving the will of God. When your obsession is to follow the leading of The Holy Spirit, there may be losses. Personal losses. You may lose friends whose love and caring you believed would last forever. Your own family may refuse to follow you into the Harvest field to achieve and complete the Assignment God has burned into your heart.

Some are teaching that the most important thing in life is your family. This is absurd. *The most important thing is to achieve the will of God,* with or without those you love.

I asked my father a few days ago, "Daddy, how do you feel when one of your children rebels against your teaching of serving the Lord?"

"One day I was quite torn apart inside," he replied slowly. As he named one of the children, he continued, "She was really away from the Lord, and I was crying out to the Lord on my face, 'Oh, what have I done wrong? Lord, I don't really know my feelings.'"

He said, "The Lord spoke quite a statement to my heart. 'Son, I have lost some of My own children, though I've done everything within My power to reach them.'"

*Do whatever God has called you to do.*

God is an achiever. He has plans, goals and dreams. He does not sit on His throne looking, feeling and hoping. He is definitely a Doer.

In fact, the first thing God did to Adam was to place him in a garden, with a job description. He was to take care of the garden.

When Jesus discussed the various people who had one talent, several talents and another who had 10 talents, He taught us. He looked at the man who produced nothing with his God-given skills and ability, and He pronounced a curse on that man.

God despises laziness. "How long wilt thou sleep, O sluggard? when wilt thou arise out of thy sleep?" (Proverbs 6:9).

He hates a sluggard. "The soul of the sluggard desireth, and hath nothing: but the soul of the diligent shall be made fat," (Proverbs 13:4).

He hates slowness to move forward.

He loves achievers so much, that He will even get involved with a rebel as long as He is attempting to accomplish something. That is how Saul became a Paul. Though he was doing the wrong thing, at least he was doing something! God responded to this desire to achieve. "And Saul was consenting unto his death. And at that time there was a great persecution against the church which was at Jerusalem; and they were all scattered abroad throughout the regions of Judaea and Samaria, except the apostles," (Acts 8:1).

Read Daniel 11:32 with me. "But the people that do know their God shall be strong, and do exploits." Paul wrote, "I can do all things through Christ which strengtheneth me," (Philippians 4:13).

Seven ingredients are necessary factors in becoming an uncommon achiever.

## *Planning*

Your desire may be to build your own home. It involves planning. When you desire your own personal business, it necessitates planning. When you write a book, it is necessary to plan.

*God is a planner.* (He is the only person I know who schedules supper 6,000 years in advance. Now, that is planning!) Jesus used an interesting illustration comparing a wise man to a fool. The wise man built his house on a rock. The foolish man built his house on sand.

"Therefore whosoever heareth these sayings of Mine, and doeth them, I will liken him unto a wise man, which built his house upon a rock: And the rain descended, and the floods came, and the winds blew, and beat upon that house; and it fell not: for it was founded upon a rock," (Matthew 7:24-25).

Creativity can *birth*.

*Planning* determines *longevity*.

Your energy *begins* a project.

Your *structure* decides its lifetime.

Jesus taught, "For which of you, intending to build a tower, sitteth not down first, and counteth the cost, whether ye have sufficient to finish it? Lest haply, after he hath laid the foundation, and is not able to finish it, all that behold it begin to mock him, Saying, This man began to build, and was not able to finish," (Luke 14:28-30).

Leaders *plan*.

Successful leaders plan *thoroughly*.

Jesus explained, "Or what king, going to make war against another king, sitteth not down first, and consulteth whether he be able with ten thousand to meet him that cometh against him with twenty thousand? Or else, while the other is yet a great way off, he sendeth an ambassage, and desireth conditions of peace," (Luke 14:31-32).

*Even ants plan.* And, they are commended for it. "Go to the ant, thou sluggard; consider her ways, and be wise: Which having no guide, overseer, or ruler, Provideth her meat in the summer, and gathereth her food in the harvest," (Proverbs 6:6-8).

*The Bible is God's personal plan book.* He discusses the plans of *past* events, His *present* plans and His *future* plans.

So do not feel guilty because you are driven and energized to achieve great goals and dreams. Be thankful. Be appreciative that the God Who created you has planted photographs of your future in the soil of your mind. Seize the moments that He energizes you to *write those dreams down,* and even share them with your closest friends.

*You were created to solve problems for others.*

Just a side thought. It is incredibly sad to be in the presence of someone who has quit dreaming, planning and imagining a future. Sorrow is when you have lost sight of a goal. "Hope deferred maketh the heart sick, but when the desire cometh, it is a tree of life," (Proverbs 13:12).

I read an interesting statistic several years ago that stated the unbelievably high percentage of retirees who die within two years of retirement—unless they find something to empty their energy, talents and passion into.

You were created for *movement.*

You were created for *accomplishment.*

You were created for a Divine *function* and purpose.

You contain an *invisible* Assignment—the problem God created *you* to solve.

The ship was not made for the harbor—it was made to *sail.*

The hammer was not made for the tool chest. It was made for building.

Your car was not made for the garage. It was made for driving.

## *5 Reasons To Plan*

It is very important for you to have a plan for your life.

It helps you *manage* your time.

It enables you to set *deadlines.*

It helps you to *qualify* people for appointments.

It enables you to avoid distractions, *protecting your focus.*

It helps you to eliminate the unnecessary and delete trivia from your daily life.

Solomon *planned* the temple. Noah *planned* the ark. Success requires more than a command from God. It requires an accurate, thorough *plan* for its accomplishment.

It takes a moment to get a *command.* It takes your lifetime to get the *plan.*

Note Joshua, the great military leader of the Israelites. He lost his first battle at Ai. He had plunged into the battle without a specific plan. He had not really heard from the Lord. He was in a flow, a momentum of winning. He became momentarily self-sufficient. He used previous victories as inspiration for his present conflict.

Every battle will require a *different* plan.

Every Assignment has a *variation* in its plan.

He lost the battle. The tragedy cost him many men that he loved. He screamed in anguish, hurt and agony before God. He is ripping his clothes off himself in despair. *Any unplanned day has the possibility of ending in tragedy.*

Successes are the *only* things planned.

Failures are never planned.

God instructed him to quit praying. Get up. Make things right. Achan had sinned. After Joshua took care of the problem through stoning Achan and his family, it left him incredibly sensitive to the *necessity of a plan.*

He stayed in the presence of God long enough to get the plan. He ambushed his enemy and succeeded—after treasuring the plan of God. *God uses plans.* Someone has said that only 3 people out of 100 plan a single day.

If you cannot plan 24 hours, you cannot plan 24 years.

If you cannot make one day produce, you cannot make your life produce. Tomorrow is not yet here. It is in the *womb.* Yesterday is over. It is in the *tomb. Life is today.*

Several years ago, I carefully analyzed the ingredients of my happiest and most exciting days. I noticed 7 ingredients were in every day that I was unusually happy. I will share some of these ingredients and factors with you for you to consider. These factors made me energized, enthusiastic, motivated, satisfied and incredibly fulfilled.

I noticed when I took the time to meticulously and carefully *write out a detailed written plan and follow it as closely as possible,* I felt good about my day. "Write the vision, and make it plain upon tables, that he may run that readeth it. For the vision is yet for an appointed time, but at the end it shall speak, and not lie: though it tarry, wait for it; because it will surely come, it will not tarry," (Habakkuk 2:2-3).

When I scheduled *two specific hours in the presence of God* for absorbing Scriptures, discussing my plans and meditating on Him, I was satisfied in an unexplainable way. "The law of Thy mouth is better unto me than thousands of gold and silver," (Psalm 119:72). "How sweet are Thy words unto my taste! yea, sweeter than honey to my mouth," (Psalm 119:103).

I noticed that my daily *telephone call to my parents* affected me emotionally. Though they lived hundreds of miles from me, I felt that my pursuit of them habitually revealed honor and respect. "Honour thy father and thy mother: that thy days may be long upon the land which the Lord thy God giveth thee," (Exodus 20:12).

Planning is not fun. It is laborious to me. It is hard. Sometimes I think to myself, "I could be getting things done instead of writing out my to-do list." We get *so busy mopping up the water that we do not have time to turn off the faucet!*

Your Assignment will only be accomplished when you take the time to discern God's plan daily. His *daily* plan for your life.

One of our most famous lawyers in America invests the first hour every day meticulously planning what the other 23 hours will produce. Think of it! He said because he had spent so much time, one complete hour, deciding carefully the value of each task of the day, when he arrived at that specific hour, he was strengthened and motivated to *complete his plan.*

# *People*

The second important ingredient in your personal achievements is *people.* God included people in *everything* He did. Smart people. Common people. Patient people. Aggressive people. Caring people. Mentors. Protégés. Friendships. Business connections. Yes, even Jesus was connected to people. He allowed them to participate in His goals and Assignment. *People were His Assignment.*

One of my closest and most treasured friends was the late, Sherman Owens, who had been an extraordinary pastor in Sarasota, Florida. He once told me, "Mike, listen to happy voices for *encouragement.* Listen to unhappy voices for *ideas."*

People contain answers.

*Unhappy customers reveal weaknesses* to every company. Great successful companies often change significantly through listening to interesting and useful complaints from unhappy employees. *Unhappy voices birth ideas,* solutions for changes. One complaining customer says, "My order took 4 weeks to arrive." So the employer says, "Find the fastest shipping transportation possible and negotiate."

*Happy* people are wonderful for *relationships.*

*Unhappy* people are marvelous resources for *ideas.*

Every person in your life has their place. It is vital that you recognize their unique and specific contribution. Why did God bring this person to you? True, some are not easy to get along with. Some are not fun. But God has a reason for them being in your life.

Carefully observe the wife of Potiphar. She lied about Joseph. She accused him of raping her. That is a horrible and terrifying false accusation. It placed him in the dungeon, in the pit, in the prison. But God used the attack on his character to *link him to his next season.* He met the butler who introduced him to Pharaoh. He found favor in the most unlikely circumstances.

There is another side of the picture. Not every person around you is placed there by God. *When Satan Wants To Destroy You, He Puts A Person In*

*Your Life.* Delilah was not sent by the Father to destroy the life of Samson. Samson went to the wrong *place,* where he met the wrong *person* who influenced him in the wrong *direction.*

*God is careful about the people He sends to you.* He sends you people who *protect your focus*...who guard your Assignment. It is important to honor and treasure the people who are like walls around your life to keep you harnessed and focused on the dreams and goals God has established for your life. *Mentors are gifts from God.* When I needed additional information and Wisdom regarding raising my son, I asked my mother. She raised 7 children. You will need financial mentors, spiritual mentors and relationship mentors. Some will nurture the greatness of God in you.

*You will need protégés.* These are those who learn from you, sit at your feet and extract what God has placed on your table. Your protégés will force you to think your *highest* thoughts. They watch your life. They *study* your reactions. Your attitudes are examined and evaluated. Your opinions are *tested.* You

need protégés because they force you to
*correct your course continually*. Whether
it is your children, friends or son-in-law,
*someone needs to be receiving from you.*

*You need friends.* Friends do not
make attempts to change you. They
attempt to *understand* you. They
permit you to move any direction you
desire. Sometimes they motivate you.
Sometimes they do not. It is important
that you have a variation of friends.

Some friends will be your *coach*—
*advising* you.

Some friends will be your
*cheerleaders—inspiring* you.

Picture a great football team.
Those football players need coaches
*correcting* them. They need
cheerleaders *coaxing* them. They need
fans—to *pay* them!

Every person has a *different* role in
your life. Do not force your cheerleaders
to develop the mentality of a coach. Do
not force your coaches to lighten up and
become your cheerleader.

Years ago, I made a major mistake.
A young lady I really loved worked for
me. She was fun. Delightful. But she
was so messy and unorganized in her

filing system, it was horrifying. She took bank statements and stuffed them in envelopes. She coded them wrong, and I felt obligated to fire her.

After she was gone, I walked into the office and could not believe the atmosphere of death that prevailed in the staff. Her presence brought such joy, energy and excitement that I had overlooked how lifeless the others were without her present. She was literally the energy of the entire office. She was the catalyst for movement among the staff. I just had her in the *wrong position.*

Husbands often want their wives to be something they cannot be. Wives sometimes want husbands to be different. Each of us has a different function, a different role and a different contribution.

Your eye does not get angry at the ear for not seeing. It does not say, "Well, if I had been on that side of your face, I would have seen the baseball coming!" Your legs do not get angry at your hands for not walking. Your hands do not get angry at your legs for not reaching.

They have *different* functions.

Your relationships require *repair, correction, restoration.* Nurture them. Feed them. Fuel them. Understand them.

## *Pain*

Pain is an important and necessary factor in achievement. Opposition is normal. Crisis is normal to a productive person.

Sometimes we wish we were God. I have heard people say, "I wish I were God. I would not hurt." Yet nobody hurts more than God. God knows pain.

Even Jesus knew pain. Pain is part of the life process. Great prophets wept. Some even wanted to commit suicide. Jeremiah cried, "Oh that I had in the wilderness a lodging place of wayfaring men; that I might leave my people, and go from them!" (Jeremiah 9:2). He would rather run a motel in Arizona than stay in the ministry!

*Pain can make you lose confidence in the people to whom you are assigned.* Micah cried, "The best of them is as a brier: the most upright is sharper than a thorn hedge:...Trust ye not in a friend," (Micah 7:4-5).

Elijah could outrun horses. He ate miracle meals brought by birds. He called down fire on water-soaked sacrifices. Yet he once became so despondent he asked God to kill him! (Read 1 Kings 19.)

Jonah, famous for "Whale University," had 120,000 converts in a single crusade. Yet later he cried out to God to take his life: "...take, I beseech Thee, my life from me; for it is better for me to die than to live," (Jonah 4:3).

The wealthy hurt. Rich and wise Solomon confessed that he came to an emotional crisis so devastating that he "hated life," (see Ecclesiastes 2:17). *Dreams require seasons.* Seasons of insignificance, incubation and isolation. Regardless of how much you love God, you will know pain.

*Any lifestyle that contains progress, produces pain.*

Fortunately, pain is seasonable. "...weeping may endure for a night, but joy cometh in the morning," (Psalm 30:5). "And let us not be weary in well doing: for in due season we shall reap, if we faint not," (Galatians 6:9).

How can you successfully handle

pain?

1. *Honestly Examine The True Cause of It.* Is your pain because of an unwise *decision* you made? An *untrustworthy person* in whom you placed confidence? A situation you created through *ignorance?*

2. *Is It Really Your Problem or Someone Else's Problem You Have Adopted For Yourself?* Mothers do this frequently. They borrow pain from their children. It does not help the child. It weakens them so that they are unable to progress in their own lives. This is unfortunate, but it happens frequently.

3. *Concentrate On The Conclusion of Your Problem, The Solution.* Pain is *not* an ending. *It is a beginning.* It is a birthing of something *significant.*

Jesus cried out in the garden of Gethsemane. It appeared that His mind was in torment. He did not really want to die that way, the way of the Cross. But for the joy set before Him, He endured the Cross. He pictured the *conclusion.* "Looking unto Jesus the Author and Finisher of our faith; Who for the joy that was set before Him endured the cross, despising the shame, and is set down at the right hand of the throne of God," (Hebrews 12:2).

Sometimes it is tempting to say to yourself, "If I pray enough, there will be no more pain. If I raise my children exactly right, there will be no more pain. If I do everything perfectly on my job, there will not be pain." Wrong. *The most perfect person on earth knew the greatest pain,* Jesus of Nazareth.

But He recognized that *pain is a passage.*

You must do the same. *Pain is discomfort created by disorder.* Pain is the proof that *something is wrong,* that corrections must be made. Pain is *not* your enemy. It is merely *the proof that you have an enemy.* Permit pain to *educate* you. Pain exposes the weaknesses of others. Pain reveals the closeness of God to your life. Pain motivates you to reach—for the only One who can perfect you, your Heavenly Father. Pain is not your destination—merely the price for arriving at your destination. Keep your focus on the conclusion...*pain is a small price for a great miracle* about to be experienced.

## *Problem-Solving*

*Everything God has made was created to solve a specific problem.* Mechanics solve car problems. Dentists solve teeth problems. Mothers solve emotional problems. Your eyes see. Your ears hear. Your feet take you places. Your hands grasp. Your mouth speaks. Your nose smells. *You are a collection of solutions.*

It is important that you find the problem God specifically created you to solve while on earth. You may not be good with numbers or talkative. But you may be a good listener. You may be great in electronics. There is something you are equipped and skilled to do—*find it.*

What you love to think about, study and discuss is a clue to your Assignment. *What You Hate Reveals Something You Were Created To Correct.* What grieves and saddens you is a clue to something you were *created to heal.*

Your *patience* will solve a problem for somebody.

Your *information* will solve a problem for another.

Your *listening* solves a problem for another.

## 5 Powerful Questions

You must find the person who has the problem you were created to solve. When you have a dream to achieve a specific goal, ask yourself these questions:

1.  **What Problem Will This Really Solve?**
2.  **Is Anybody Else Already Solving This Kind of Problem?**
3.  **What Can I Possibly Do That Has Not Been Done By Someone Else?**
4.  **Am I The Only Person In My Area Who Can Solve This Problem?**
5.  **Is There Someone Else Anywhere Who Is Capable of Solving This Specific Problem?**

Always remember that *your income is determined by the problems you solve.* Money is merely a *reward* for solving a problem. When you see someone who has great wealth, they have done something that solved a problem for other people.

## *Patience*

*Patience is a Seed.* It is a Seed of time that you plant to grow a particular Harvest. Any great achievement involves time. It took God hundreds of years to produce what He wanted in a family. He is patient with millions of rebellious and disobedient people every day. He is patient with egotistical atheists, glib-tongued philosophers, religious Pharisees and know-it-all teenagers. Yet His Seeds of patience are not wasted. You have reached for Him because of His patience.

*Patience is the willingness to assign Time to work on a solution.* In *your* life. In the life of *others* close to you.

Patience produces exceptional friendships.

Patience produces great marriages.

Patience will produce what money cannot produce.

Patience has turned around weak and unhealthy people through exercise and focus, producing powerful, strong bodies.

"The Lord is good unto them that wait for Him, to the soul that seeketh

Him. It is good that a man should both
hope and quietly wait for the salvation of
the Lord," (Lamentations 3:25-26). "Wait
on the Lord: be of good courage, and He
shall strengthen thy heart: wait, I say,
on the Lord," (Psalm 27:14).

*Wait* for seasons to end. "For the
vision is yet for an appointed time, but
at the end it shall speak, and not lie:
though it tarry, wait for it; because it
will surely come, it will not tarry,"
(Habakkuk 2:3).

### *3 Rewards of Waiting*

▶ Waiting *reveals the weaknesses* of impatient enemies.
▶ Waiting *provides God time* to
  interrupt any attack on your
  life with a miraculous
  deliverance.
▶ Waiting gives time for *others
  to become* what Wisdom is
  producing within them.

### *Power*

The sixth ingredient in achieving a
goal is *power*—the ability to accomplish
an objective.

Jesus promised power, capability

and enablement. "But ye shall receive power, after that the Holy Ghost is come upon you," (Acts 1:8).

The Holy Spirit empowers you. "That He would grant you, according to the riches of His glory, to be strengthened with might by His Spirit in the inner man," (Ephesians 3:16).

You must permit that power to work within you. "Now unto Him that is able to do exceeding abundantly above all that we ask or think, according to the power that worketh in us," (Ephesians 3:20).

Do not trust your own strength. "Trust in the Lord with all thine heart; and lean not unto thine own understanding. In all thy ways acknowledge Him, and He shall direct thy paths. Be not wise in thine own eyes: fear the Lord, and depart from evil. It shall be health to thy navel, and marrow to thy bones," (Proverbs 3:5-8).

*Consult The Holy Spirit Consistently.* He walks beside you. He loves you. He nurtures you. He knows exactly what you need. Ask Him, "Walk with me. Give me the enablement. Lord, how do I handle this particular problem today?" Ask His advice. Consult Him on every single decision of your life. Consult Him in discerning the motives, true intentions and character of those around you.

The Holy Spirit will give you *pictures* for the gallery of your mind to *meditate* upon. Abraham had a *picture* of his future generations. Joseph had a *picture* of himself in the palace. Jesus had a *photograph* of Himself going through the Cross and to the resurrection.

What you look at the longest becomes the strongest in your mind. Get a picture of Jesus. "Looking unto Jesus the Author and Finisher of our faith; Who for the joy that was set before Him endured the cross, despising the shame, and is set down at the right hand of the throne of God," (Hebrews 12:2).

## *Prosperity*

Prosperity is *having enough of God's provision to complete His Assignment for your life.* It is not luxury. It is a necessity. Some think it is nice cars and a large home. Prosperity is provision sufficient to complete a command from The Holy Spirit.

It is the will of God for you to prosper. "Beloved, I wish above all things that thou mayest prosper and be in health, even as thy soul prospereth," (3 John 1:2).

God wants you to have good things. "No good thing will He withhold from them that walk uprightly," (Psalm 84:11).

Provisions are the product of obedience. "And all these blessings shall come on thee, and overtake thee, if thou shalt hearken unto the voice of the Lord thy God," (Deuteronomy 28:2).

Disobedience will birth losses and tragedies. "If ye be willing and obedient, ye shall eat the good of the land: But if ye refuse and rebel, ye shall be devoured with the sword: for the mouth of the Lord hath spoken it," (Isaiah 1:19-20).

*When you solve problems, you will be rewarded financially.* It is the plan of God. Money should never be your goal, merely your *weapon.* It is a *tool.* It is *not* a destination. It is a *vehicle* to help you arrive at a destination. It is an *instrument for the achiever.* Money is not the goal of a true achiever, but a tool to create the dream God has placed within you.

## *3 Keys To Prosperity*

▶ *Spending* money *wisely* is an important key.

▶ *Saving* money *habitually* is a major key.

▶ *Sowing* money *expectantly* is the master key to multiplication.

When you give to men, it comes back. "Give, and it shall be given unto you; good measure, pressed down, and shaken together, and running over, shall men give into your bosom. For with the same measure that ye mete withal it shall be measured to you again," (Luke 6:38).

When you give to God, it comes back one hundred times. "Verily I say unto you, There is no man that hath left house, or brethren, or sisters, or father, or mother, or wife, or children, or lands, for My sake, and the gospel's, But he shall receive an hundredfold now in this time, houses, and brethren, and sisters, and mothers, and children, and lands, with persecutions; and in the world to come eternal life," (Mark 10:29-30).

Sow *obediently*.
Sow *consistently*.

Sow *generously.*
Sow *expectantly.*
*What you respect will always come toward you.*

These are the 7 Ingredients in becoming the achiever God created you to be.

### Our Prayer Together

"Precious Holy Spirit, thank You today for my special friends reading this special book, giving (or offering) wonderful revelation on *The Mentor's Manna On Achievement* to unlock the greatness in their hearts and lives. Thank You for enabling us to *complete* our Assignment on earth and do *great exploits.* We shall begin today with total abandonment to Your commands for our life. In the precious name of Jesus. Amen."

It is very important that you *share this book* with a friend. Review your personal notes that you have written with *those who matter to you* and anyone else who is experiencing a problem in achieving their dreams.

# DECISION

## Will You Accept Jesus As Your Personal Savior Today?

The Bible says, "That if thou shalt confess with thy mouth the Lord Jesus, and shalt believe in thine heart that God hath raised Him from the dead, thou shalt be saved," (Romans 10:9).

Pray this prayer from your heart today! *"Dear Jesus, I believe that You died for me and rose again on the third day. I confess I am a sinner...I need Your love and forgiveness...Come into my heart. Forgive my sins. I receive Your eternal life. Confirm Your love by giving me peace, joy and supernatural love for others. Amen."*

☐ Yes, Mike, I made a decision to accept Christ as my personal Savior today. Please send me my free gift of your book *31 Keys to a New Beginning* to help me with my new life in Christ.

NAME _____

ADDRESS _____

CITY _____ STATE _____ ZIP _____

PHONE ( _____ ) _____ E-MAIL _____

DFC

*Clip & Mail*

*Mail To:* **The Wisdom Center**
4051 Denton Hwy. · Fort Worth, TX 76117
1-817-759-BOOK · 1-817-759-2665 · 1-817-759-0300
**You Will Love Our Website..! WisdomOnline.com**

Unless otherwise indicated, all Scripture quotations are taken from the King James Version of the Bible.
*The Mentor's Manna On Achievement* · ISBN 1-56394-045-0/B-79
Copyright © 1996 by **MIKE MURDOCK**
All publishing rights belong exclusively to Wisdom International
Editor/Publisher: Deborah Murdock Johnson
Published by The Wisdom Center · 4051 Denton Hwy. · Fort Worth, Texas 76117
1-817-759-BOOK · 1-817-759-2665 · 1-817-759-0300
**You Will Love Our Website..! WisdomOnline.com**